Usborne
BIG
STICKER BOOK OF
SHARKS

Illustrated by
Amanda Shufflebotham

Written by **Alice James**

Designed by
Helen Cooke and **Josephine Thompson**

With expert shark advice from
Hettie Brown at the **Shark Trust UK**

Contents

At the back of this book, you will find lots of stickers.

The sharks in this book are not drawn exactly to scale.

Cold oceans

Sharks are big FISH.
Some of them are strong, vicious
PREDATORS, with razor-sharp teeth and
strong, muscular bodies. Fill this ocean with
sharks and their prey – the creatures they
eat. Add a huge great white shark leaping
up out of the cold water.

Underwater forest

This is a KELP FOREST. Kelp is a huge type of seaweed that grows in the ocean. Add in lots of leopard sharks swimming through the wafting kelp.

Beautiful reefs

Some sharks prefer warm, shallow coral reefs to cold, wide, open ocean. Add all sorts of sharks to make this bright coral reef bustle with life.

Hammerheads

These curious creatures are hammerhead sharks. Their wide eyes make them experts at sensing the world around them. During the day they hang out in big gangs of up to a hundred. Add a group here.

Their odd, long heads are called cephalofoils.

Eggs and babies

If you look under the sea really closely you might see little eggs containing tiny baby sharks. They're called mermaid's purses. Add mermaid's purses onto this seabed, and baby sharks too.

Not ALL sharks lay eggs. Some give birth to babies.

Baby zebra sharks look different from adults. As they grow up their stripes fade and they turn spotty.

Fish friends

Some sharks have close friendships with fish – they help each other out. Tiny remora fish clean parasites and dirt off bull sharks. In return, they get food and protection.

At this special underwater cleaning station, dozens of little wrasse fish clean reef sharks all over, from their skin to their teeth.

Gentle giants

Not all sharks hunt their prey. Some just swim along while their wide mouths suck in gallons of water, fish and krill. These sharks are called filter feeders and they are usually VERY BIG.

Whale sharks are the BIGGEST FISH in the ocean.

Glow-in-the-dark sharks

Down in the murky depths of the ocean are sharks
that live in the dark. Sunlight doesn't reach this far,
so these creatures make their own light.

Closest relatives

Rays are closely related to sharks. They're mostly flat, but come in lots of patterns and sizes, from small spotted eagle rays to ENORMOUS manta rays.

The BIGGEST sharks

Millions of years ago, a huge shark called the MEGALODON swam through Earth's oceans. Scientists don't know exactly how big it was, but they think it was the biggest predator of all time.

Build a megalodon across these pages. Match the stickers to the patches here.

You'll need to use several stickers
because it's so enormous!

This is the size of a great white shark today,
to show just HOW big a megalodon was.

Safe in the trees

These trees growing straight out of the water are called mangroves. Baby lemon sharks hide safely in the tangle of mangrove roots.

They're called lemon sharks because their skin has a yellow tinge.

Spot the sharks

Here are some of the sharks in this book, showing how big they are compared to each other. Add a sticker for each of them.

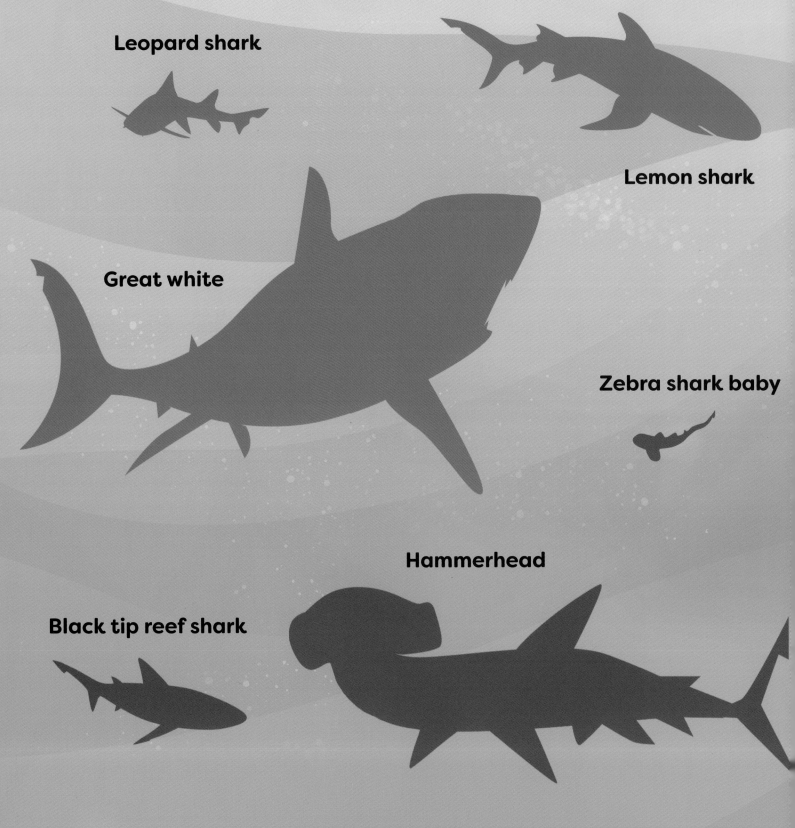

Leopard shark

Lemon shark

Great white

Zebra shark baby

Hammerhead

Black tip reef shark

With additional design by Johanna Furst and digital manipulation by Nick Wakeford